D1400938

SPORTS ALL-STARS

STEPHEN CURRY

Eric Braun

Lerner Publications • Minneapolis

Lerner Publications Company
A division of Lerner Publishing Group, Inc.
241 First Avenue North
Minneapolis, MN 55401 USA

For reading levels and more information, look up this title at www.lernerbooks.com.

Main body text set in Albany Std 15/22. Typeface provided by Agfa.

Library of Congress Cataloging-in-Publication Data

Names: Braun, Eric, 1971– author.
Title: Stephen Curry / Eric Braun.
Description: Minneapolis : Lerner Publications, [2017] | Series: Sports All–Stars | Includes bibliographical references and index. | Audience: Ages: 7–11. | Audience: Grades: 4 to 6.
Identifiers: LCCN 2016029323 (print) | LCCN 2016030609 (ebook) | ISBN 9781512425833 (lb : alk. paper) | ISBN 9781512431230 (pb : alk. paper) | ISBN 9781512428285 (eb pdf)
Subjects: LCSH: Curry, Stephen, 1988-—Juvenile literature. | Basketball players—United States—Biography—Juvenile literature.
Classification: LCC GV884.C88 B73 2017 (print) | LCC GV884.C88 (ebook) | DDC 796.323092 [B] —dc23

LC record available at https://lccn.loc.gov/2016029323

Manufactured in the United States of America
1-41351-23295-9/26/2016

CONTENTS

No Doubt 4

Shooting Star 8

All about Overload 12

Regular Guy 16

It's Raining Threes. 22

All-Star Stats 28

Source Notes 29

Glossary 30

Further Information 31

Index 32

NO DOUBT

Curry (center) shoots against Memphis Grizzlies guard Beno Udrih (right) during the 2015 NBA playoffs.

Maybe when the 2015 National Basketball Association (NBA) playoffs began, there were still doubters. Stephen Curry was too small. He wasn't athletic enough. He would never be one of the greats. Curry had heard those doubts all his life.

The **point guard** had just set the record for most **three-pointers** in a season (286) and led the Golden State Warriors to a 67-win season. His team was one of the favorites to win it all. Yet still people doubted Curry could be a superstar in the NBA.

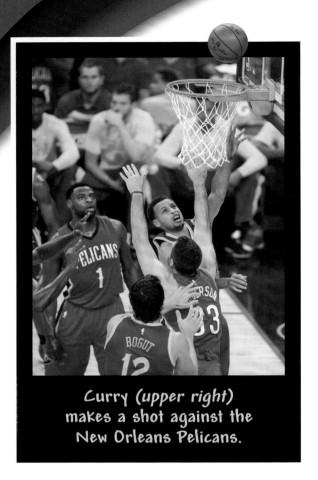

Curry (upper right) makes a shot against the New Orleans Pelicans.

In the playoffs, he began to knock down the doubts like long-distance three-pointers. Consider game 3 in the first playoff round against the New Orleans Pelicans. The Warriors were down by 20 points in the fourth quarter before Curry led a dizzying comeback. In the final seconds, he dodged a **defender** and launched a long shot from the corner of the court. Two huge defenders crashed down on him as he let the ball go. But the three-pointer went in, and the game was tied. The Warriors went on to win in overtime.

Or consider game 4 against the Memphis Grizzlies in the second round. Memphis had won two games in a row and held a 2–1 edge in the series. Curry started game 4 by scoring 21 points in the first half to set the tone of the game—and change the tone of the series. Golden State went on to win the series 4–2.

Most important, consider the 2015 NBA Finals against the Cleveland Cavaliers. The Cavaliers jumped out to a 2–1 series advantage. Then Warriors coach Steve Kerr made a lineup change that helped open up the court for Curry. He scored 22, 37, and 25 points, respectively, in the last three games of the Finals—all Warriors wins.

As Curry celebrated winning the NBA championship with his team, he may have thought about everything he'd done that year. Three-point record. NBA Most Valuable Player (MVP) award. World champ. Basketball fans no longer doubted Curry's greatness. He'd just had one of the best seasons in NBA history. But that was only the beginning. Next year was going to be out of this world.

Cleveland Cavaliers guard Iman Shumpert (*right*) tries to block a shot against Curry (*left*) in game 5 of the 2015 NBA Finals.

Dell Curry tries to slip past a Boston Celtics defender during a 1999 game.

Dell Curry was an NBA three-point specialist from 1987 to 2002. Like many parents, he taught his son Stephen to play the game he loved. Unlike other parents though, Dell's son grew up to be the greatest shooter in the world.

Growing up, Stephen Curry practiced his shot on a rickety hoop behind his grandpa's house in North Carolina. The hoop was at the edge of the woods. Missed shots bounced into the mud or, worse, bounced into the bear-infested woods. So Curry learned not to miss.

As a teen, Curry could already light up the scoreboard. He scored so much in one game that his dad had to leave the building. "I felt bad for the other team," Dell said. "I couldn't watch what he was doing to those kids."

Stephen Curry launches a shot for his high school team, the Knights.

Curry was a scoring machine. Still, the big college teams didn't call. They thought he was too short. Too thin. He settled on a small school in North Carolina called Davidson College.

When Curry was a sophomore, he broke the national record for three-pointers in a season and took his small school to the **NCAA tournament**. They made it all the way to the **Elite Eight**. Opponents began to cover him with more than one defender. He still lit up the scoreboard. His shooting became must-see entertainment. Even NBA superstar LeBron James flew into town just to watch him play.

The next year, Curry led the nation in scoring. The Golden State Warriors took him with the seventh

Two Duke defenders try to block Curry from making a shot.

Curry with his parents after being selected by the Golden State Warriors in the first round of the NBA draft.

pick in the 2009 NBA draft. But there were still a lot of questions. Was he worth such a high pick? History is full of guys who were great in the NCAA but flopped in the NBA.

Early in his career, the questions seemed valid. Curry was good—not great. But in 2014, the Warriors hired a coach, Steve Kerr, who changed how the team played. He installed a high-energy style that relied on lots of ball movement—and player movement. The style suited Curry's game and helped him thrive. He became more than just the best shooter in the game. He became an MVP. And the Warriors went on to be the 2015 champs.

Curry shoots a three-pointer against the Orlando Magic.

Early in his NBA career, Stephen Curry injured his ankle. He had surgery to repair it. Then he hurt it again. And had surgery again. This may have been the best thing to happen to him.

While rehabbing his second injury, he met a new trainer who showed him an unusual training method. Since he could not put weight on his ankle, he worked on **ball handling** while seated. Curry would dribble a basketball while catching a tennis ball thrown at him. He would dribble one heavy basketball and one regular ball at the same time. Or he would dribble one ball normally while passing another between his legs.

Curry's training helps him get better control of the ball.

Dribbling two basketballs at once is a way for Curry to get in the zone before a game.

According to Curry, the idea is to "overload" his senses. It's sort of like rubbing your belly and scratching your head at the same time. But dribbling two balls at the same time is way harder.

Many fans have seen Curry dribble two basketballs at once before games. The ritual is about more than improving his skills or giving the fans a good show. It's just one more way of overloading his senses. This kind of practice mimics what a point guard has to do during a game—dribble, watch the defenders, set up a play, and more—all at the same time.

One of the weirdest **drills** Curry does involves hi-tech goggles. The goggles flash lights in his face from different angles, creating gaps in what he can see. His mind has to fill in the rest. With the goggles on, he does ball-handling drills. Another drill involves a board of flashing lights. He quickly touches the lights as they fire up on a board—while he's dribbling, of course.

Many point guards work hard to stay at the top of their game. But Curry is the best player in the NBA at the position. That's because he has taught himself to do two things at once better than most players can do one.

Curry takes a shot with two Oklahoma City Thunder defenders guarding him.

REGULAR GUY

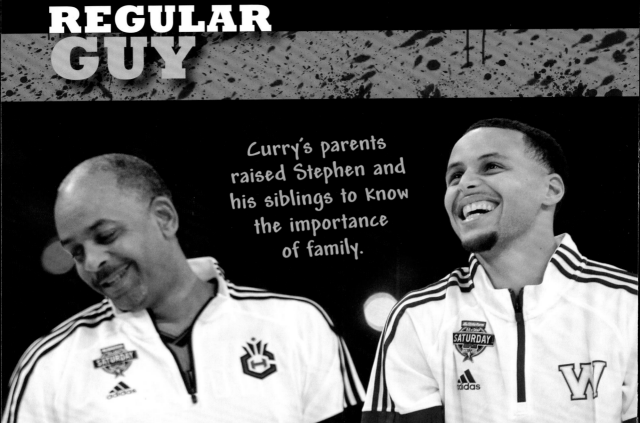

Curry's parents raised Stephen and his siblings to know the importance of family.

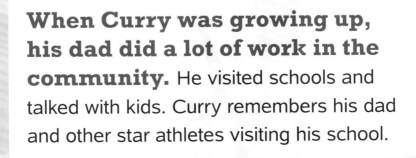

When Curry was growing up, his dad did a lot of work in the community. He visited schools and talked with kids. Curry remembers his dad and other star athletes visiting his school.

When Stephen Curry was a kid, he starred in a Burger King commercial with his dad.

He remembers how much it meant to him. "I know how happy me and my friends were at that age to see somebody we looked up to come and spend some time," he said.

Curry has carried on his father's work. He has a passion for kids. Even while his team was going for the all-time wins

Stephen Curry's family, along with his wife and daughters, is known as the First Family of the NBA.

Curry greets students at a 2016 Junior NBA Day event.

record in the 2015–2016 season, he visited schools. He talks with students about living a healthful lifestyle and making smart choices. He regularly visits children through the Make-A-Wish Foundation. It makes him as happy as it does them.

In 2011, Curry married his longtime girlfriend, Ayesha Alexander. They have two daughters. Riley was born in 2012, and Ryan was born in 2015. Curry often brings Riley with him to interviews after games. Video clips show a patient dad. He answers questions as his daughter goofs around and steals the attention. In interviews and on the court, Curry is hard to fluster.

Many celebrities are careful to keep their personal life private. They don't talk about their family or beliefs

Curry's older daughter, Riley, likes to be in the spotlight during press conferences.

Curry and his wife, Ayesha, attended the
2015 Teen Choice Awards together.

publicly. But Curry is comfortable sharing what he is really like. He talks openly about his religion and family. It's all part of what makes Curry easy to relate to. For a superstar, he seems like a regular guy.

Under Armour

Like most pro athletes, Curry endorses sports brands. He used to have a deal with Nike, but that ended in 2013. When Curry met with the company to talk about a new contract, he was not yet an MVP or a huge star. The company didn't seem to value him. They even said his name wrong and offered him less money than other players. Curry signed a deal with Under Armour instead.

Curry has designed a number of shoes for Under Armour.

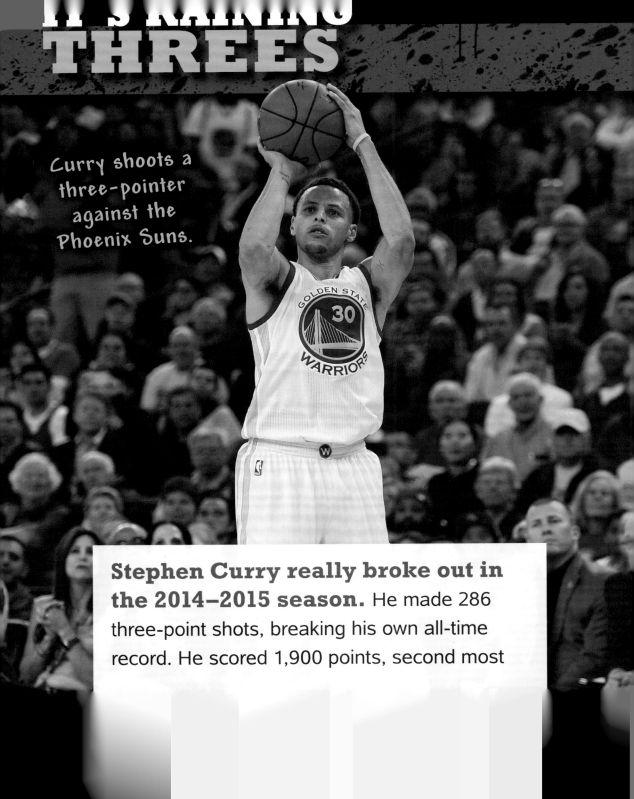

THREES

Curry shoots a
three-pointer
against the
Phoenix Suns.

Stephen Curry really broke out in the 2014–2015 season. He made 286 three-point shots, breaking his own all-time record. He scored 1,900 points, second most

Curry (center right, first row) and his teammates pose with the 2015 NBA Finals trophy after defeating the Cleveland Cavaliers.

in the league. He averaged 7.7 assists per game, also coming in at sixth best. He was named the league MVP. And then Curry led his Warriors against LeBron James and the Cavaliers to win the NBA championship.

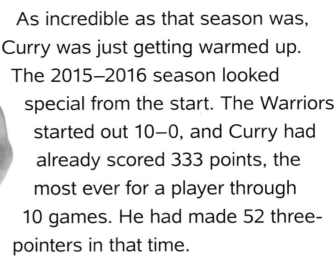

As incredible as that season was, Curry was just getting warmed up. The 2015–2016 season looked special from the start. The Warriors started out 10–0, and Curry had already scored 333 points, the most ever for a player through 10 games. He had made 52 three-pointers in that time.

As the winter wore on, Curry kept sinking threes. And the Warriors kept winning. They went 24–0 before losing for the first time on December 12 to the Milwaukee Bucks. By then, it was clear the Warriors had a great chance at breaking the Chicago Bulls' 1995–1996 record of 72 wins in a season. And Curry was almost certain to break his own record for three-pointers.

And then, on February 27, 2016, it happened. With a record of 41–17, the Warriors' opponent, the Oklahoma City Thunder, was no pushover. But Curry torched them for 46 points and 12 three-pointers. That gave him 288 three-point baskets on the season, breaking his old record of 286.

Here's the really amazing part: There were still 22 games left to play. It was the fastest a single-season record had ever been broken in any sport. By the end of the season, Curry had made a total of 402 three-pointers.

Curry drives the ball into the hoop against the Portland Trail Blazers.

He scored more threes than most *teams* in NBA history.

The Warriors went on to break the single-season NBA record by winning their 73rd game on the last day of the season. It felt almost like an afterthought compared to Curry and his three-point record.

Of course, athletes play for championships, and they still needed to win the playoffs. The Warriors were the top-ranked team and the favorites to repeat as

LeBron James (center) celebrates with the Cleveland Cavaliers after winning the 2016 NBA championship.

LeBron James was emotional about bringing the NBA title home to Ohio since he was born in Akron, near Cleveland. Yet Curry was born in the same city—and in the same hospital—as James.

champions. They made it to the Finals again—and again faced James's Cavaliers. The Warriors took a 3–1 series lead. But then, Cleveland came back to win the title. The final game was a nail-biter that Cleveland won, 93–89. Curry scored 17 points and made only four of his 14 three-point shots.

"It hurts, man," Curry said after the game. But he promised to remember the hurt and use it to drive him to improve next year. An improved Curry could well be a scary thought for the rest of the league.

All-Star Stats

The all-time leaderboard for most three-pointers in a season is heavy on Curry. It's Curry, then Curry, and later it's more Curry.

Most Three-Pointers in an NBA Season

402 Stephen Curry, Golden State Warriors (2015–2016 season)

286 Stephen Curry, Golden State Warriors (2014–2015 season)

276 Klay Thompson, Golden State Warriors (2015–2016 season)

272 Stephen Curry, Golden State Warriors (2012–2013 season)

269 Ray Allen, Seattle SuperSonics (2005–2006 season)

267 Dennis Scott, Orlando Magic (1995–1996 season)

261 Stephen Curry, Golden State Warriors (2013–2014 season)

257 George McCloud, Dallas Mavericks (1995–1996 season)

243 Jason Richardson, Charlotte Bobcats (2007–2008 season)

240 Peja Stojakovic, Sacramento Kings (2003–2004 season)

How early in the season have other record-breakers hit their records?

League	Player	Record	Percentage of Season Remaining
MLB	Barry Bonds	Home runs	1.3
NHL	Wayne Gretzky	Points	1.3
NFL	LaDainian Tomlinson	Touchdowns	18.8
NBA	Wilt Chamberlain	Points	23.8
NBA	Stephen Curry	Three-pointers	29.3

Source Notes

9   Scott Davis, "How Stephen Curry Became the Best Shooter in the NBA," *Business Insider*, June 4, 2015, http://www.businessinsider.com/how-stephen-curry -became-best-shooter-in-the-nba-2015-6.

17 Associated Press, "Stephen Curry Is Setting Standard on and off the Court," *USA Today*, April 11, 2016, http://www.usatoday.com/story/sports /nba/2016/04/11/stephen-curry-is-setting-standard -on-and-off-the-court/82902510/.

27 SI Wire, "Stephen Curry, Draymond Green React to Warriors' NBA Finals Loss," *Sports Illustrated*, last modified June 21, 2016, http://www.si.com /nba/2016/06/20/nba-finals-stephen-curry-draymond -green-react-warriors-loss-cavaliers.

Glossary

ball handling: controlling the ball with skillful dribbling

defender: a player who defends the team's basket and tries to prevent the opposing team from scoring

drills: physical or mental exercises that are practiced regularly

Elite Eight: the fourth round of the NCAA basketball tournament, with only eight teams remaining

NCAA tournament: a tournament held each year to determine a champion for college basketball's top level

point guard: the basketball player who usually leads the team when it has the ball and is trying to score

three-pointers: shots made from beyond the three-point line

Further Information

Bay Area News Group. *Golden Boys: The Golden State Warriors' Historic 2015 Championship Season*. Chicago: Triumph Books, 2015.

Fishman, Jon M. *Stephen Curry*. Minneapolis: Lerner Publications, 2016.

Golden State Warriors
http://www.nba.com/warriors/

Savage, Jeff. *LeBron James*. Minneapolis: Lerner Publications, 2016.

Sports Illustrated editors. *Sports Illustrated Kids Big Book of Who Basketball*. New York: Time Home Entertainment, 2015.

Stephen Curry
http://www.nba.com/playerfile/stephen_curry

Index

Chicago Bulls, 24
Cleveland Cavaliers, 7, 23, 27
Curry, Ayesha Alexander, 18
Curry, Dell, 8–9, 16–17
Curry, Riley, 18–19
Curry, Ryan, 19

Elite Eight, 10

Golden State Warriors, 5–7,
    10–11, 23–24, 26–27

James, LeBron, 10, 23, 27

Kerr, Steve, 7, 11

Make-A-Wish Foundation, 18
MVP award, 7, 11, 21, 23

NBA playoffs, 5–6, 26
Nike, 21

Oklahoma City Thunder, 24–25

training drills, 13–15

Under Armour, 21

Photo Acknowledgments

The images in this book are used with the permission of: © iStockphoto.com/
iconeer (gold and silver stars); © iStockphoto.com/ulimi (black and white stars);
© epa european pressphoto agency b.v./Alamy, p. 2; Spruce Derden/USA Today
Sports/Newscom, p. 4; Stephen Lew/Cal Sport Media/Newscom, p. 6; JOHN G.
MABANGLO/EPA/Newscom, pp. 7, 22; Lee K. Marriner/UPI Photo Service/Newscom,
p. 8; Seth Poppel Yearbook Library, pp. 9, 17; Chuck Liddy/MCT/Newscom, p. 10; AP
Photo/Paul Sakuma, p. 11; © McClatchy-Tribune/Tribune Content Agency LLC/Alamy,
p. 12; AP Photo/Ben Margot, p. 13; AP Photo/Rick Bowmer, p. 14; Kevin Jairaj/USA
Today Sports/Newscom, p. 15; AP Photo/Frank Franklin II, p. 16; AP Photo/Chris
Young, p. 18; MONICA M. DAVEY/EPA/Newscom, p. 19; PG/Splash News/Newscom,
p. 20; Shingo Ito/AFLO/Newscom, p. 21; LARRY W. SMITH/EPA/Newscom, pp. 23,
24; AP Photo/David Blair/CALSP, p. 25; Gary A. Vasquez/REUTERS/Newscom,
p. 26.

Front cover: © epa european pressphoto agency b.v./Alamy (Stephen Curry),
© iStockphoto.com/neyro2008 (motion lines), © iStockphoto.com/ulimi (black and
white stars), © iStockphoto.com/iconeer (gold and silver stars).

DATE DUE

			PRINTED IN U.S.A.